W9-BEG-102

Fredericksburg
The Official Guide

Researched and Compiled by the
Historic Fredericksburg Foundation, Inc.

THE
DONNING COMPANY
PUBLISHERS

All research, photography, narratives, timelines, and mapping were completed by the Historic Fredericksburg Foundation, Inc., staff and members of the Publication Committee.

Front cover photo blend:
Left: *1857 Bird's Eye (updated in 1862 to show Civil War damage)*. Courtesy Library of Congress.
Right: *Modern Aerials/Bird's Eye. Looking Northwest.* Courtesy Allen Schmidt.

Copyright © 2014 by Historic Fredericksburg Foundation. Inc.
The Lewis Store
1200 Caroline Street
Fredericksburg, VA 22401
www.hffi.org

All rights reserved, including the right to reproduce this work in any form whatsoever without permission in writing from the publisher, except for brief passages in connection with a review. For information, please write:

The Donning Company Publishers
184 Business Park Drive, Suite 206
Virginia Beach, VA 23462

Steve Mull, *General Manager*
Barbara B. Buchanan, *Office Manager*
Richard A. Horwege, *Senior Editor*
Brett Oliver, *Graphic Designer*
Kathy Adams, *Imaging Artist*
Lori Porter, *Project Research Coordinator*
Nathan Stufflebean, *Research and Marketing Supervisor*
Katie Gardner, *Marketing Assistant*

Dennis N. Walton, *Project Director*

Library of Congress Cataloging-in-Publication Data

Fredericksburg : the official guide / compiled and edited by the Historic Fredericksburg Foundation, Inc. ; illustrations and cartography by Carthon W. Davis, III ; introduction by John Hennessy.
    pages   cm
    ISBN 978-1-57864-882-5 (soft cover : alk. paper)
 1. Fredericksburg (Va.)—Guidebooks. 2. Historic sites—Virginia—Fredericksburg—Guidebooks. 3. Historic buildings—Virginia—Fredericksburg—Guidebooks. I. Historic Fredericksburg Foundation (Fredericksburg, Va.)
    F234.F8F78 2014
    975.5'366—dc23
                                                                          2014020042

Printed in the USA at Walsworth Publishing Company

TABLE OF CONTENTS

ACKNOWLEDGMENTS

Fredericksburg: The Official Guide would not have been possible without the efforts of many individuals. The genesis of this book lies in the *Handbook of Historic Fredericksburg, Virginia*, authored by venerable local historians Barbara Pratt Willis and Paula S. Felder and published by the Historic Fredericksburg Foundation, Inc. (HFFI) in 1993. Recognizing the continued need for a local guidebook, the HFFI Publications Committee commenced work on this new publication, partially relying on the scholarship of Willis and Felder while imbuing the existing narrative with important new research and sharing information on several additional locales with our readers.

The Publications Committee is indebted to Willis and Felder for their original compilation. Their *Handbook* stood for many years as the only volume of its kind, providing details on many notable people and places for locals and visitors alike. We hope that both authors are honored by our attempts to continue their research.

This book was compiled and edited by Kerri Barile (Publications Committee Co-Chair), Linda Billard, Carthon Davis III (Publications Committee Co-Chair), Loretta Lettner, John Hennessy, Jerrilynn Eby MacGregor, Sean Maroney (HFFI Executive Director), Sara Poore, Bill Shorter, Scott Walker, and Barbara P. Willis. Carthon Davis III completed all photography and served as the project cartographer. He also organized the historical images used in this book. University of Mary Washington interns Frances Womble and Carol Quinn assisted the team in this endeavor. This guide was entirely a collaborative effort, and we are extraordinarily thankful for everyone's contributions.

The City of Fredericksburg and both Stafford and Spotsylvania Counties kindly allowed HFFI to use cartographic data from their Geographic Information System (GIS) as the basis for the pullout map.

This new publication would also not have been possible without generous grants and donations from several key players, including the City of Fredericksburg, the Duff McDuff Green Fund, and Dovetail Cultural Resource Group. We deeply appreciate their immense support of Fredericksburg-area preservation and HFFI's outreach and education efforts.

INTRODUCTION
By John Hennessy

Every community has a history, but only a few have a history that reverberates beyond its local confines, across the American landscape. Fredericksburg is such a place.

Home to founders, host to giants, witness to war, and setting for both slavery and freedom, Fredericksburg is a metaphor for the Southern, and indeed American, experience. For more than a century before the Civil War, the town and surrounding community pursued prosperity relentlessly—seeking it in part through the labor of enslaved African Americans. The Civil War brought destruction and dislocation rarely equaled across the South, and the postwar period witnessed immense social change in a community that reflected classic small-town America for the next century.

Fredericksburg was one of four Virginia towns founded on the Fall Line (the upper limits of navigation) along Virginia's major rivers: Alexandria on the Potomac, Richmond on the James, Petersburg on the Appomattox, and Fredericksburg on the Rappahannock. Of the four, Fredericksburg was the slowest to grow. Between its founding in 1728 and the Civil War, Fredericksburg grew to be a place of just five thousand souls, one-third of them slaves. Its economy depended first on the riverside port facilities along Sophia Street. Later, as economic activity sprawled across Virginia's Piedmont region, Fredericksburg turned to the area to the west as a profit source. At various times, the town invested in a turnpike, canal, plank road, and railroad, all of them tending westward and southward, seeking to encourage shipment of goods through Fredericksburg's port.

While town leaders constantly looked outward in search of prosperity, local residents built a vibrant economy of their own. Caroline Street was, until the 1970s, the preeminent retail address between Washington and Richmond. William Street was the locale of warehouses and light industries that have since transformed into shops and restaurants. Princess Anne Street was conceived as the town's cultural center. The spectacular Circuit Courthouse, five churches, the town's nineteenth-century theater, Town Hall (with its European-style Market Square), and some of the most beautiful residences in Virginia lined the surrounding streets. Many still remain.

Located in the heart of downtown at 706 Caroline Street, the Visitor Center provides information and literature on the activities and history of Fredericksburg and the surrounding region.

Fredericksburg was a place of historic importance before many of Virginia's towns even found their place on a map. George Washington grew up across the river at Ferry Farm, and his mother spent the last two decades of her life at her home on Charles Street. (Indeed, it was Mary Washington, not her son George, who brought Fredericksburg most of its worldwide fame before the Civil War.) Thomas Jefferson wrote the Statute for Religious Freedom at Weedon's Tavern on Caroline Street. James Madison visited often. James Monroe lived in Fredericksburg for several years, serving on the Town Council. In fact, few towns in America can boast a more impressive procession of political punditry over the decades: at least twenty-seven sitting, past, or future presidents have visited Fredericksburg, along with a future King of England (in 1860) and Winston Churchill (in 1929).

The Civil War exacted a heavy toll on Fredericksburg. Few places in America suffered longer or more variously. The town was occupied, bombarded, looted, and fought over for more than two years. At least one hundred buildings succumbed to fire, bombardment, demolition, or vandalism. Thousands of white residents became refugees, seeking shelter wherever they could find it—with strangers, friends, family, or even in distant cities and towns.

While the town and its white residents suffered, the war prompted the greatest social change in the region's history: the end of slavery. In the town and surrounding counties, about half the population was enslaved before the war. Thousands refused to wait for the formal issuance of the Emancipation Proclamation in 1863 and fled bondage into Union lines during the spring and summer of 1862—one of the largest, most concentrated flights to freedom of the war. Many others waited for war's end to travel the figurative road to freedom. Whether a white resident or black, free or enslaved, the Civil War was the fulcrum upon which this community's history turns. Everything in Fredericksburg happened either "before the War" or after it—and a dialogue on which war is never required.

It took decades for the Fredericksburg region to recover from the Civil War. The economic boom it perpetually sought would not materialize until the advent of Interstate 95 in the 1960s. Meanwhile, Fredericksburg continued its contentious relationship with the Rappahannock, which periodically unleashed damaging floods. Over time, the river became less central to the town's economy, and it was the motorcar that helped sustain the area's economy as a tourist destination and an important wayside on the trip southward along Route 1 from Washington, D.C. Late in the twentieth century and into the twenty-first, the Fredericksburg region grew exponentially. By 2011, the city's population exceeded twenty-two thousand. With the surrounding counties of Stafford and Spotsylvania, the region boasts nearly a quarter of a million residents.

Towns—and their sense of community—have long been a hallmark of American life. Across the United States, towns and communities are disappearing into a morass of boundary-less suburbs. While Fredericksburg has witnessed its necessary share of growth and change, it is a rare place where the heart of a community still beats. More than 230 antebellum buildings survive downtown. Community organizations, some decades and centuries old, still thrive. Each street in the historic downtown area still fulfills the function it has for centuries: Sophia Street, the functional waterfront; Caroline, the hub of retail; Princess Anne, the city's cultural center. Today, the places our predecessors built for life, work, and worship help give this community an enduring identity—a constancy that both distinguishes Fredericksburg and sustains it.

This book is about those places, but it is more than that. It is the collective work of a community that cares about itself. We hope that by reading these pages and walking our town's streets, you will see, as we who live here do, that both Fredericksburg and history matter, that what happened here in the past reverberates still across the American land-scape with a clarity that enlightens, humbles, and inspires us all.

A BRIEF CHRONOLOGY OF FREDERICKSBURG

11,000 B.C. Native American Paleo-Indians occupy the Fredericksburg region, living in nomadic bands that travel for food and shelter.

8000 B.C. During the Archaic Period, Indian groups develop seasonal campsites along the Rappahannock River, which are revisited yearly to harvest local flora and fauna and exploit riverine resources.

1200 B.C. Native Americans begin to settle in long-term villages along the river, erecting permanent dwellings and crafting local pottery.

1608 John Smith explores the Rappahannock River north to the present-day location of Fredericksburg, an area previously inhabited by various Indian tribes, including the Secobeck.

1671 A deed of sovereignty (Buckner-Royston patent) is granted by Governor William Berkeley to John Buckner and Thomas Royston; the waterfront portion of their patent contained a small cluster of buildings known as the Leaseland, later renamed Fredericksburg.

1681 Major Lawrence Smith erects a fort just south of the present-day location of Fredericksburg to encourage permanent settlement in the area.

1714 Fort Germanna is established by Lieutenant Governor Alexander Spotswood on the Rapidan River as the seat of his enterprise. Settlement begins westward expansion from the Leaseland.

1720 Spotsylvania County is created by the General Assembly with a Courthouse at Germanna.

1728 Fredericksburg and nearby Falmouth are established by act of the General Assembly; Fredericksburg is named for Prince Frederick and the town's streets are named for members of the royal family.

1730 Fredericksburg is named an official receiving and inspection station for tobacco.

1732 County Court of Spotsylvania is moved from Germanna to Fredericksburg; a Courthouse and Jail are erected on Princess Anne Street.

1734 First Anglican church is erected in town; named St. George's after the surrounding parish.

1738 George Washington arrives at his family's new home across the river from Fredericksburg, a parcel now known as Ferry Farm.

1738 Agricultural Fair is established in Fredericksburg, the oldest agriculturally based fair in the United States.

1759 Fredericksburg is expanded by an act of the General Assembly. The new boundaries included present-day Dixon, Winchester, and Canal Streets.

1777 Thomas Jefferson and other members of the General Assembly's "Laws Committee" meet at Weedon's Tavern on Caroline Street to discuss and draft Jefferson's Statute of Religious Freedom, a precursor to the United States Constitution's Bill of Rights.

1782 Fredericksburg is chartered as an incorporated town by the General Assembly.

1787 *Virginia Herald*, one of the earliest newspapers in Virginia, begins publication in Fredericksburg.

1794 Robert Brooke of Fredericksburg is elected governor of Virginia.

1807 A great fire sweeps through Fredericksburg, destroying about half the buildings in the downtown area.

1812 Although citizens prepare for the worst, the town escapes damage during the War of 1812.

1824 General Lafayette, French hero of the American Revolution, is entertained for two days here on his triumphant tour of the United States.

1835 At the time of publication of the *Virginia Gazetteer*, Fredericksburg had more than 3,000 residents: 1,797 white, 1,124 enslaved, and 387 free blacks. It also had five churches, more than a dozen schools, four taverns, two newspapers, and many small businesses.

1837 The Richmond, Fredericksburg, and Potomac Railroad arrives, bisecting the downtown area and permanently changing area transportation.

1851 Fredericksburg is again expanded by act of the General Assembly. The new boundaries included present-day Summit Street, Sunken Road, and Pelham Street.

1853 The Fredericksburg and Orange Railroad is founded, seeking to provide transportation to communities west of town.

1861 War erupts in nearby Manassas; over the course of the four-year war, Fredericksburg changes hands by Union and Confederate troops eleven times.

1862 First Battle of Fredericksburg is fought December 11–15.

1863 Second Battle of Fredericksburg is fought May 2–4 as part of the Chancellorsville Campaign.

1865–1870 Fredericksburg is under the military jurisdiction of the United States government.

1879 Partially as a result of Reconstruction-era population growth, Fredericksburg becomes an incorporated city.

1912 Fredericksburg becomes the second city in America to adopt the Council-City Manager form of government.

1930 Sylvania Industrial Corporation opens just south of the city, a massive cellophane plant that provided employment for many residents during the Great Depression.

1942 In October, a massive flood envelops a large portion of downtown, forcing hundreds of families from their home and damaging bridges and roads throughout the area.

1946 Route 1 Bypass is completed, diverting through traffic away from the historic downtown area for the first time in 250 years.

1955 Interstate 95 is designed through Virginia, providing the first major transportation change since the arrival of the railroad 120 years earlier.

1955 Historic Fredericksburg Foundation is established in response to the demolition of numerous important buildings, including the home of naval hero Matthew Fontaine Maury.

1960 Seeking equal rights, Fredericksburg African American residents conduct a "sit-in" at three downtown eating establishments—W. T. Grant's, F. W. Woolworth's, and Peoples Service Drug Store—all once located near the intersection of Caroline and William Streets.

1971 A forty-block area of downtown is placed on the National Register of Historic Places as the Fredericksburg Historic District.

1980 Fredericksburg becomes part of the International Sister City Program, establishing an association with Frejus, France. Sister City alliances would later be created with Prince's Town, Ghana, and Schwetzingen, Germany.

1984 Fredericksburg Historic District is expanded to include the myriad Colonial Revival-styled buildings throughout downtown.

1984 The city annexes additional land from Spotsylvania County to encompass an area measuring 10.5 square miles.

1992 Virginia Rail Express is established, with Fredericksburg as one of its two termini, opening the region to occupancy by a wave of Washington, D.C. commuters.

2010 City Council passes Fredericksburg's first Historic Preservation Plan.

2011 Fredericksburg commences a celebration of the sesquicentennial of the Civil War, with tens of thousands of visitors flocking to the city to help commemorate the 150th anniversary of the war. Commemorative events span 2011 through 2015, with special programs dedicated to the major battles that took place in our region: the First and Second Battles of Fredericksburg, the Battle of Chancellorsville, and the Battle of the Wilderness.

2013 Fredericksburg City Council votes to erect a new Courthouse to be constructed at the intersection of Princess Anne and Charlotte Streets.

1

CAROLINE STREET COMMERCIAL DISTRICT

For more than two centuries, Caroline Street (known as Main Street for most of its existence) was the shopping mecca for residents of the Fredericksburg region, be they brought by cars, horses, trains, or carts. While William Street (known at one time as Commerce Street) housed businesses and the occasional warehouse, Caroline was the town's retail center, selling everything from the latest European fashions to bat guano. The Town Council fought constantly to keep Caroline and

The corner of Caroline and William Streets—the commercial heart of the Fredericksburg region for two centuries.

neighboring streets pleasant for visitors and shoppers, urging nineteenth-century residents to stop dumping refuse in the street and trying to persuade residents to keep hogs off the pavement.

Parades, presidents, protesters, and Santa Claus have all frequented Caroline Street. In the eighteenth century, George Weedon kept his tavern at the corner of Caroline and William Streets, where he entertained some of the greatest men of Revolutionary America, including Thomas Jefferson and George Washington. One-hundred-and-eighty-five years later, in a department store a few doors away, more recent patriots conducted Civil Rights-era sit-ins, seeking equality under the very laws forged by Jefferson and Washington. In the twentieth century, Caroline Street assumed the aspect of a classic American downtown. Two theaters (the buildings still stand) offered the latest movies; the soda fountain at Goolrick's Drugstore dispensed (and still does) milk shakes and malts, and nearby department stores offered virtually everything residents of the Fredericksburg region needed (though you can no longer get guano).

Not surprisingly, given its antiquity, the street has experienced a variety of disasters, resulting in a greatly modified landscape. Much of the upper end of Caroline Street above Hanover Street was destroyed in the Great Fire of 1807, which is why most buildings were rebuilt using brick. Later, most of the 1000 block on

the east side of the street was destroyed again in the bombardment of December 1862. Despite these events, most of Caroline Street retains the character—and the vibrancy—it has had for most of two centuries.

Little has changed at the intersection of Caroline and William Streets thanks to the foresight of city officials, preservation groups, and private citizens. (Library of Congress)

2

THE CITY AND CONFEDERATE CEMETERIES
Corner of William and Washington Streets

From the outside, this burial ground appears as one entity. (Certainly the elegant archway with "Confederate Cemetery" upon it would suggest so.) But, in fact, inside the brick wall at the head of Amelia Street are two cemeteries—each with a distinct story and, initially, purpose.

In 1844, town leaders arranged for the purchase of an old cornfield at this location to create a new town cemetery "for the decent interment of the dead."

A gate that still stands on William Street went up, and by 1860, more than 150 townspeople

The Confederate Cemetery—to the right of the gate—emerged in the years after the Civil War. More than thirty-three hundred Confederate soldiers are buried here, including five generals.

The City Cemetery, created in 1844, was the burial ground for some of Fredericksburg's most prominent families into the twenty-first century.

Containing the graves of local residents and soldiers together, all enclosed by the same brick wall, the City and Confederate Cemeteries are indistinguishable to most.

were buried there. By then, a visitor remembered that the cemetery was "regularly laid off . . . the walks being graveled, and the plats covered with a rich carpet of greenwood and adorned with many a fragrant shrub and flower." The overall effect, wrote this observer, "was pleasing in the highest degree."

In 1865, in the wake of a Civil War that left the region scarred with graves and destruction, the Ladies' Memorial Association (LMA) of Fredericksburg sought to create a distinct and honored place for the burial of Confederate dead. The LMA approached the Fredericksburg Cemetery Corporation to discuss a merger and expansion of the existing cemetery. The merger never happened, but the expansion did. The LMA acquired several acres just beyond the north wall of the Fredericksburg Cemetery. By 1870, more than thirty-three hundred Confederate dead had been disinterred from area battlefields and reburied here. When the LMA discovered it had more land than it needed for Confederate burials, it started selling off land to townspeople. Over time, the physical distinction between the two cemeteries was lost.

Today, everything to the left of the Amelia Street gate is the City Cemetery; everything to the right is the Confederate Cemetery. Scattered throughout both are six Confederate generals and a thousand stories of a community facing trial and triumph over the decades.

3

CITY DOCKS
Foot of Sophia Street

The bucolic set of docks and waterfront pedestrian paths visible today suggests a longtime public use of the city dock area. This landscape, though, is recent—a late-twentieth-century creation that masks an extensive and dynamic history. In the eighteenth century, the town wharf provided the first public river docks in the area. In fact, Thomas Jefferson recounted in his diary that the navigable Rappahannock appeared twelve feet deep at Fredericksburg.

By the early nineteenth century, the wharf had become a bustling port. Numerous stores, industries, and residences lined both sides of what was then known as Water Street, and goods were exported on large ships harbored in the deep channel. By 1828, a new steamboat line made regular trips to the wharf, providing convenient transportation for both merchandise and passengers. Rocky Lane continued to provide access from the riverfront to the surrounding neighborhood.

The Civil War had a profound impact on the wharf, as it did on the entire town. During a May 1862 visit to the area, President Abraham Lincoln crossed here

For its first 150 years, the docks on Sophia Street were Fredericksburg's major connection to the outside world. Everything from sailing ships to steamboats docked here.

on a "canal boat bridge" constructed during a Union occupation of the city. Then, in December of that year, during the Battle of Fredericksburg, Union troops under the command of General Ambrose Burnside crossed the Rappahannock on a pontoon bridge located at this site.

This cobblestone street connected the town docks to lower Caroline Street. Before the war, slaves often passed this way to board ships carrying them away. During the Civil War, Union soldiers swarmed up the street towards Confederate troops waiting on Marye's Heights.

At the turn of the twentieth century, the area along the river was marked by the industrial activities typical of a port town. Standard Oil Company maintained two large storage tanks, a garage, a warehouse, and an office building at the end of the street. A little farther up stood a brewery, a lumber house, and a canning factory. After this industrial heyday, all of lower Sophia Street was abandoned during the mid-twentieth century. It was not until the late-1970s that the town dock was reborn.

4

FREDERICKSBURG CITY COURTHOUSE
815 Princess Anne Street

Holding court in various forms has been at the heart of Fredericksburg's rhythms for virtually its entire history. Since the mid-nineteenth century, Fredericksburg has been graced with one of the most compelling Courthouses in all of Virginia. James Renwick, Jr., who received $300 for his services, designed the building at 815 Princess Anne Street in 1852. The sum seems modest in light of his credentials. In 1846, Renwick designed the new Smithsonian Building in Washington, D.C.—known today simply as "the Castle." He would go on to design the magnificent St. Patrick's Cathedral in New York City in 1858—now one of the most-visited houses of worship in North America.

The people of Fredericksburg handily approved by referendum the idea of a new Courthouse (the vote tally was 170 to 112), but they balked at the cost of constructing Renwick's design: $13,850, to be paid to local builder William Baggot. Citizens rounded up 172 signatures for a petition against Renwick's creation, instead favoring a simpler $6,000 building. Council rejected the protest, and in 1852, city officials cut the ribbon on a brick masterpiece (which has almost

Fredericksburg's Courthouse, designed by famed architect James Renwick, is distinguished for its Gothic Revival style.

During the Civil War, the Fredericksburg Courthouse was used as Confederate barracks, Union signal station and hospital, and as temporary housing for escaped slaves. (National Park Service)

always been covered with a faux exterior—be it stucco or faux sandstone). Over the years, the building has served other purposes in addition to its court duties, such as a library, fire department, and boxing venue.

Its courtly rhythms have been interrupted in a significant way only once: during the Civil War. In 1861, the Confederates used the basement as a barracks. In the summer of 1862, the Union Army housed escaping slaves in the Courthouse before sending them northward, to freedom. The building also served as a hospital (as did most of Fredericksburg's public buildings)—several vivid accounts of its use in that capacity exist. And just after the war, the Courthouse hosted the Freedman's Court, which adjudicated the cases of former slaves.

Today, the building stands as one of the finest Gothic Revival Courthouses in the mid-Atlantic and the only one in Virginia. For 150 years, it has been a physical and iconic anchor for our community.

5

FREDERICKSBURG BAPTIST CHURCH
1019 Princess Anne Street

The Fredericksburg Baptist Church traces its roots to 1767, when it was known as the Upper Spotsylvania Church. The first church in town was on the site of the present-day train station on Lafayette Boulevard. Formally organized as an independent church in 1804, the church later moved to Sophia Street in 1818; it expanded in 1820. In the late 1830s, the church built its first brick structure.

Originally an integrated congregation with segregated seating, the church experienced tensions as mid-century approached. With an increasing congregation of approximately eight hundred members (three-fourths of whom were African American), a plan for splitting the church was proposed in the early 1850s. The church began to raise money to help fund the split.

Under the leadership of the Reverend William F. Broaddus, the church split in 1855. The African American members kept the Sophia Street location, which later became Shiloh Baptist Church (Old Site). The white congregation moved to the Fredericksburg Baptist Church's present-day location at 1019 Princess Anne Street.

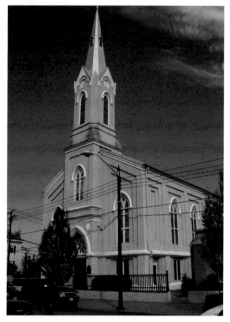

The new church for white parishioners was constructed on its current site in 1855 in the Gothic Revival style. Reverend Broaddus formed the Fredericksburg Female Academy (1855–1862) in the new church basement, where young women learned English, Latin, French, and music. Schooling came to a halt in December 1862 when the church held its last service until after the Civil War.

The Fredericksburg Baptist Church, constructed in 1855. Owing to growth, the church has expanded several times over the years, including the adaptation of an Art Deco movie theater building facing Caroline Street.

As with many churches in the area, the Union Army used the building as a field hospital. By war's end, the structure was significantly damaged. After the war, members of the church arranged for the structure to be restored, and the congregation continued to grow. The church building was expanded in 1898, 1910, 1950, 1972, and 1990, as a result of the increasing size of its congregation.

http://www.fredericksburgbaptistchurch.org/

Just six years old when the Civil War began, the Fredericksburg Baptist Church saw hard times— its pews destroyed, walls riddled with bullets, and interior used as a hospital. (National Park Service)

6

FREDERICKSBURG METHODIST CHURCH
308 Hanover Street

Methodists first organized in the area following late-eighteenth century visits by circuit-riding preachers, such as Bishops Francis Asbury (buried nearby in Spotsylvania County) and Thomas Coke. Reverend John Kobler established the formal congregation in 1803. Kobler's home, in the 400 block of Hanover, was long used as the church's parsonage and today houses church pastoral staff, making it the oldest Methodist property still in use in the Virginia Conference of that denomination. Typical of many nineteenth-century Protestant denominations, the Methodist Church split over the issue of slavery, producing two Methodist buildings in the city until the congregation reunited in 1866.

The main section of this Gothic Revival-styled building dates to 1882, replacing a building that was heavily damaged during the Civil War. Incidentally, the federal government twice refused (most recently, in 1985) to compensate the church for damage wrought during the Civil War. The interior was used both as a hospital and a stable. Not many usable furnishings remained after the Union Army left.

In the nineteenth century, there were three Methodist churches in town, including Fredericksburg's first church solely for African-Americans. Today, the Fredericksburg Methodist Church is only surviving Methodist church in downtown. (*The History of the City of Fredericksburg, Virginia* by S. J. Quinn, 1908)

The current main building has many additions and wings (including one added in 2008—which had to conform to local design guidelines because it lies within the Downtown Historic District), yet maintains an active, downtown congregation in its original location.

This is the third church on this site, built in 1888. Before the Civil War, the congregation split over the issue of slavery, and the current building was erected for the remaining congregation in the post-war years.

One of its expansions includes the nineteenth-century brick house next door, which has been incorporated into one of the additions. In particular, visitors should note the bell tower, restored to its nineteenth-century design.

http://www.fumcva.org/

7

FREDERICKSBURG PRESBYTERIAN CHURCH
810 Princess Anne Street

The Presbyterian Church in Fredericksburg was organized in 1808. Originally located at Amelia and Charles Streets on land donated by Mrs. Ann Patton, daughter of General Hugh Mercer, the church moved to its present location on Princess Anne Street in 1833. The Greek Revival-styled structure is one of the two oldest church buildings in the city.

Overseeing the establishment of the church, Pastor Samuel B. Wilson led the congregation from its founding until 1841, during which time membership rose to nearly five hundred people. Many members came from the local Episcopal Church, unsatisfied with its current state. Wilson also started a Sunday school, believed to be the first in Virginia.

During the Civil War, members of the church donated the bell to the Confederacy. The building sustained heavy damage during the conflict and became a hospital for wounded soldiers. Clara Barton, who would later start the American Red Cross, nursed soldiers at both the Presbyterian and Episcopal

Though battered by the Civil War, the Presbyterian Church and other downtown congregations remained a foundation of the Fredericksburg community. Seven of eight wartime congregations still exist. (Library of Congress)

Built in 1833, the Presbyterian Church is Fredericksburg's oldest church building. Its congregation led many charitable efforts, including the founding and construction of the Female Orphan Asylum in what is today a private resident known as Smithsonia.

Churches. One hundred years later, on September 25, 1962, her efforts were marked by a ceremony and a bronze marker placed in the churchyard.

Immediately after the Civil War, on May 10, 1865, a group of women formed the Ladies' Memorial Association of Fredericksburg—the first in the South—in the church basement. The group first raised funds to buy a new bell to replace the one donated to the Confederate cause. Money was then raised for the formation of a cemetery for fallen Confederate soldiers. Construction of the cemetery began in 1871, under the guidance of Thomas Walker Gilmer, a veteran of the Army of Northern Virginia. In 1882, Mr. S. Graham Howison and Mr. Edgar M. Crutchfield started a Sunday school for African American children at the church. They continued their mission to educate and care for area youth by operating the Fredericksburg Female Orphan Asylum through the early twentieth century. The congregation remains active today.

http://fredericksburgpc.org/

8

FREDERICKSBURG TRAIN STATION
200 Lafayette Boulevard

On January 23, 1837, local residents gathered at the city's new passenger station, excitedly awaiting the arrival of the first Richmond, Fredericksburg, and Potomac train and the dawning of a new era in transportation. Since that momentous day, the railroad has continued to play an important role in shaping Fredericksburg's future, and the city's railway station has remained an integral part of the downtown landscape. Ironically, this same excitement and reliance on rail led to the destruction of the tracks—and indeed the town around it—during the Civil War, as both Union and Confederate troops valiantly fought for control of this all-important resource. Like the town, the rail and passenger station were soon rebuilt, returning vibrancy to the downtown area.

By the early-twentieth century, the late-nineteenth century train station was in poor repair. A new station was commissioned in 1909. This new $125,000 facility included a new passenger depot and a set of raised tracks, thus allowing traffic to flow under the rail. Completed in 1910, the new Colonial Revival–style station was constructed by noted local builder E. G. "Peck" Heflin.

As originally built in 1910, the rail tracks in Fredericksburg were at street level. They were not raised to their current location until 1927, when increased automobile traffic made at-grade tracks problematic.

Described as "one of the handsomest and best equipped stations in the State" by the *Fredericksburg Daily Star*, the new building featured chestnut accents, terrazzo floors, and both electric and gas lights. As a sign of its time, it also had separate, fully equipped "white" and "colored" waiting rooms.

Rail continued to thrive in Fredericksburg until the 1950s, when the completion of the new I-95 highway ushered in an era of high-speed automobile traffic, diverting travelers from the core of town. It was not until 1992 and the arrival of the Virginia Rail Express commuter system that the rail system regained prominence. The train station has been restored to reflect its original Colonial Revival design, including its pressed tin ceiling on the interior. Today, hundreds of travelers use the historic rail station and the restaurant within each day, reviving the centuries-old tradition of train travel in Fredericksburg.

Today's station retains many of the architectural characteristics on display when the building first opened to the public in 1910. (*Fredericksburg Daily Star*, 1910)

9

FREDERICKSBURG WAR MEMORIAL
Intersection of George and Liberty Streets

The memorial to honor the men and women who served and died defending our nation was dedicated on June 1, 1926, eight years after the World War I Armistice. Alongside the Roll of Honor was placed a symbol of that war, a captured German howitzer. In 1942, that trophy again contributed to the machinery of war—this time donated as scrap metal, which was desperately needed by a U.S. industry that was mobilizing for World War II. Another symbol of that war, a twin 40mm antiaircraft gun mount, obtained by American Legion Post 55 from Marine Corps Base, Quantico, was placed at the site in 1962. Over the years, the memorial site has added a lighted flag and, most recently, a monument with granite pillars that bears the names of the fallen from all of the wars.

Nearby is a bronze plaque that pays tribute to fifty-one Confederate soldiers who died during the months prior to the Battle of Fredericksburg and were buried in the Barton Street Cemetery. A companion marker denotes the nearby location of a cemetery site for free and enslaved members of the African American community.

The War Memorial records the names of Fredericksburg residents who sacrificed their lives while fighting for the United States of America.

Dedicated in 1926, the War Memorial proudly defines George Street. (Suzanne Carr Rossi, *Fredericksburg Free Lance-Star*)

10

GENERAL HUGH MERCER MONUMENT

Richmond has Monument Avenue. Washington, D.C., has the Mall. Fredericksburg has Washington Avenue—a picturesque corridor with a ceremonial lawn and monuments commemorating people, places, and events notable in our history. One of the most prominent landmarks along Washington Avenue is the General Hugh Mercer Monument.

Hugh Mercer, a general in the Revolutionary War, died of wounds suffered at the Battle of Princeton in 1777. He was a doctor who had fled Scotland after the Battle of Culloden in 1746, where he had supported the efforts of the heirs of the House of Stuart to reclaim the thrones of England and Scotland. The following year, he moved to Pennsylvania and continued his medical practice. He fought, and was badly wounded, in the French and Indian War. Moving to Fredericksburg in 1760, he practiced medicine until joining Washington's forces in 1775. After being appointed a brigadier general in 1776, his forces took part in the renowned Christmas attack after crossing of the Delaware River and were prominent in battles at Trenton and Princeton, New Jersey. General Mercer died of wounds received at Princeton and was interred in the Laurel Hill Cemetery in Philadelphia.

After George Washington, General Hugh Mercer is Fredericksburg's most prominent Revolutionary hero, killed at the Battle of Princeton in 1777. The statue of him on Washington Avenue was dedicated in 1906.

Inscription found on the monument.

The bronze statue of General Mercer was erected in 1906 by the United States government. The sculptor was Edward Virginius Valentine of Richmond, who created the famous recumbent statue of Robert E. Lee at Washington and Lee University.

Formal dedication plans for the unveiling of the statue were made and then forgotten. In April 1987, after the statue had been in place for more than eighty years, the City of Fredericksburg and the Hugh Mercer Chapter of the Sons of the American Revolution organized a formal dedication ceremony. As further tribute to General Mercer, seven states—Virginia, Pennsylvania, Ohio, Kentucky, Illinois, Missouri, and New Jersey—have counties named in his honor.

11

HUGH MERCER APOTHECARY SHOP
1020 Caroline Street

Hugh Mercer was a Scottish-trained doctor (and political refugee) who came to Fredericksburg in 1760. Ten years later, he opened an apothecary shop (the equivalent of a modern-day pharmacy) near this spot in 1771. This eighteenth-century building replicates his apothecary and medical practice, which actually was located in the next block of Caroline Street. The museum building was originally a residence.

At his apothecary, curative potions for various ailments were prepared using local herbs, spices, and materials. Even oyster shells were ground up to provide stomach-settling calcium. One mixture was so strong that a sip of it would supposedly "cheer a good man with a bad wife," as advertised in city papers. In his medical practice, Mercer—typical of eighteenth-century doctors—sought to totally purge his patients of their illnesses. Bleeding was prominent as a curative process and, even today, large, live medical leeches are on display.

Mercer married, settled down in Fredericksburg, and raised a family, eventually answering the American call-to-arms by serving his friend George Washington as one of his generals during the Revolutionary War. He died as a result of wounds received at the Battle of Princeton. His descendants became a vital part of the nation's cultural and military history, including Johnny Mercer, a popular songwriter in the mid-twentieth century, and the renowned World War II general, George S. Patton.

This eighteenth-century building houses a museum of medicine and apothecary, recalling the role of Hugh Mercer before the Revolution. A Scottish immigrant, Mercer opened a medical practice in Fredericksburg in 1760.

For decades, Preservation Virginia operated the Hugh Mercer Apothecary Shop. Founded in 1889 as the Association for the Preservation of Virginia Antiquities, the organization is the oldest statewide preservation group in the United States. For more than one hundred years, the organization has fulfilled its mission to "preserve, promote and serve as an advocate for the state's irreplaceable historic places for cultural, economic and educational benefits of everyone." The property was transferred to the Washington Heritage Museums in 2013, which are the current stewards of the building and its collection.

The Hugh Mercer Apothecary remembers Mercer as a physician, pharmacist, leader, and soldier. Exhibits include eighteenth-century treatments, including leeches and snakeroot. (Washington Heritage Museums)

http://www.washingtonheritagemuseums.org/

12

HURKAMP PARK
Corner of William and Prince Edward Streets

Before the plot of land known as Hurkamp Park served the City of Fredericksburg in a recreational capacity, it served the community in another way—as a repository for the dead. St. George's Church, which was affiliated with the Church of England for most of the eighteenth century, acquired the property in 1774 to build a new church and cemetery. At the conclusion of the American Revolution, however, the Church of England lost its official standing in Virginia, and town leaders annexed the property for a public burial ground.

For almost seventy years, the cemetery provided a resting place for prominent citizens and those of less-assuming social positions. Although burials continued to take place through 1853, this particular "final" resting place turned out to be not so final. By 1875, few of the graves were being maintained, and the cemetery had a decided air of neglect. To counter (or perhaps capitalize on) that problem, the City Council decided to convert the public burial ground into a public park. Before that dramatic change could be effected, however, the artifacts of burial—headstones and other monuments—were removed. The bodies remained.

Once a burial ground, the site of Hurkamp Park was cleared of grave markers in the 1870s and turned into a community green space.

Hurkamp Park was named for German immigrant John G. Hurkamp, the owner of a tannery on the town's outskirts. Hurkamp's tannery was one of Fredericksburg's few true export businesses in the 1800s—regularly shipping to customers in Europe.

The newly constituted park, which opened to the public on July 12, 1881, was named for a prominent local business-man, John G. Hurkamp. Actively involved in com-munity affairs, Hurkamp was instrumental in see-ing that the land bounded by William, Prince Edward, and Hanover Streets was transformed from a place dedicated to the dead into a place for the living to gather and socialize.

During the last years of his life, Hurkamp resided at 406 Hanover Street. Although the house is not open to the public, visitors can see a cast-iron gate that bears the Hurkamp name from the sidewalk. When Hurkamp died in 1886, he was buried in the City Cemetery, just a few blocks away from the park named in his honor.

Today, Hurkamp Park offers area residents and visitors a picturesque setting for lively outdoor concerts and a thriving farmers' market. One remnant of the former cemetery still exists: a brick wall, built in 1824, that marks the western boundary of the property.

13

JAMES MONROE MUSEUM AND MEMORIAL LIBRARY

908 Charles Street

This museum houses items and papers of our fifth president, James Monroe. A native of nearby Westmoreland County, Monroe left college to serve with Washington during the Revolutionary War and was wounded at the Battle of Trenton. He moved to Fredericksburg in 1786 to open a practice of law. He began his political career by serving on the City Council and was a trustee of the Fredericksburg Academy. In addition, he represented Fredericksburg in the Virginia Assembly and served as a member of the Virginia Convention to ratify the Federal Constitution in 1788. Monroe then moved to Albemarle County and began his rise to national prominence. He served as governor of Virginia, U.S. senator, and U.S. minister to France, England, and Spain. He went on to be secretary of state, secretary of war, and a two-term president of the United States.

The James Monroe Museum, established by his descendants in 1927, is housed in a circa 1814 building that stands on a lot once owned by Monroe. Filled with memorabilia and furnishings passed down through Monroe's family, the exhibits include Monroe's china, silver, jewelry, porcelain, and clothing as well

James Monroe moved to Fredericksburg in the late 1780s and opened a law practice in a building that stood near this site. In 1927, the James Monroe Library and Museum opened in this building as a monument to the former president.

as thousands of books, documents, maps, manuscripts, and newspapers dating to the Colonial and Federal periods. Many pieces were purchased in Paris when Monroe was United States emissary to France. The Louis XVI furniture on display was used while Monroe was in the White House. Visitors can also see two portraits of Monroe by Rembrandt Peale. A bronze bust of Monroe by Margaret French Cresson presides over the museum's Memorial Garden. Today, the James Monroe Museum is a property of the Commonwealth of Virginia, and the University of Mary Washington oversees its operation.

Today the James Monroe Museum features perhaps the greatest collection of Monroe artifacts and papers anywhere, including this Masonic apron. Generally, Masons are buried in their aprons, though with Monroe's death in New York City and the apron in Virginia, he was laid to rest without it. (James Monroe Museum and Memorial Library)

http://www.umw.edu/jamesmonroemuseum/

14

KENMORE (LEWIS PLANTATION)
1201 Washington Avenue

Local merchant Fielding Lewis constructed this brick residence in the 1770s for his second wife, Betty Washington, sister of George. The late Georgian design of both the main house and the entire grounds of the estate is iconic. The ceilings and fireplaces contain some of the finest colonial decorative plasterwork in the country.

Lewis, a native of Gloucester County, arrived in Fredericksburg in about 1745, groomed by his father, John, for a merchant's career. He prospered in that endeavor and became one of the town's leading (and wealthier) citizens. His storehouse provided supplies for George Washington during the French and Indian War. During the Revolutionary War, he was one of the principal managers of the Fredericksburg Gun Manufactory, sacrificing his personal assets

Restored in the 1920s, Kenmore stands as a testament to eighteenth-century architecture, nineteenth-century farming, and twentieth-century historic preservation in Fredericksburg.

to maintain its operations and supply weapons to the Continental Army.

Although Lewis died in December 1781, for the next fifteen years, his widow, Betty, managed the eleven-hundred-acre estate. Despite strained finances, she entertained many town leaders, especially when her famous brother came to visit, and created an elaborate sunken garden.

Not to disappoint on the interior, artists created plaster masterpieces on the ceilings of Kenmore's formal rooms. (George Washington Foundation)

In 1796, Betty Lewis moved to a farm in Spotsylvania County and died the following year. The Lewis plantation was sold in 1799, and the estate was then gradually subdivided. In 1819, Samuel Gordon purchased the house and immediate grounds and named the mansion "Kenmore," the moniker still used today.

Kenmore is now owned and operated by the George Washington Foundation, which also owns and administers the Washington Farm ("Ferry Farm") across the river. Portions of the gardens and other exterior elements were restored as a gift from the Garden Club of Virginia.

http://kenmore.org/

One of the first tasks completed during the early-twentieth century restoration was the removal of a large, arcaded addition that once stood on the north side of the building (Library of Congress)

15

LEE DRIVE AND THE FREDERICKSBURG BATTLEFIELD

For decades the Fredericksburg community and Civil War veterans had clamored for a National Military Park for Fredericksburg and the surrounding battlefields. By the 1920s, many locals had concluded it would never happen. That perception rendered the opening of Lee Drive on November 11, 1931, all the more significant. Lee Drive was the first manifestation of the still-new federal National Military Park at Fredericksburg. Its opening marked the beginning of a process of park building that has continued steadily over the past eighty years.

Citing the date of dedication (October 1928) by President Calvin Coolidge, this stone marker greets visitors at the entrance of Lee Drive.

Lee Drive—bisected into North Lee and South Lee Drives by the crossing of Lansdowne Road—was the first park road, built along a substantial part of the Confederate line at Fredericksburg. Remnants of infantry trenches (many of them built after the actual battle) and artillery positions line the road, as does Lee's headquarters post at what in 1862 was called Telegraph Hill, today Lee's Hill. Today, the road is

Ironically once the barren grounds of a war-torn landscape, today, Lee Drive provides residents and visitors a welcomed reprieve from a busy lifestyle.

an anomaly in burgeoning Fredericksburg, tree-lined and still quiet, meandering its way southward to a historical climax at Prospect Hill. Near Prospect Hill on December 13, 1862, Union troops actually broke the Confederate lines, putting the outcome of the battle momentarily in doubt for the Confederates. Soldiers came to call this end of the line "Dead Horse Hill."

Few monuments mark the Fredericksburg battlefield, but perhaps the most interesting (and certainly the largest) is the so-called "Meade Pyramid." The monument was sponsored by the women of the Confederate Memorial Literary Society and built by the Richmond, Fredericksburg, and Potomac Railroad, which runs beside it. The monument's design is modeled after the memorial to Confederate dead at Hollywood Cemetery in Richmond. Though the pyramid was likely not built to commemorate the attack of George Gordon Meade's Union division at Fredericksburg, it does in fact mark its location, and so over time has become known as the "Meade Pyramid." It is now surrounded by National Park Service land, visible from Prospect Hill, but virtually inaccessible because of the railroad tracks beside it.

At the entrance of Lee Drive stands the memorial commemorating the dedication of the park in 1928 by President Calvin Coolidge.

http://www.nps.gov/frsp

Though now inaccessible owing to train tracks, the placement of "Meade's Pyramid" was ideal at the time because trains were the preferred method of travel, offering passersby a unique sight. (National Park Service)

16

LEWIS STORE
(HISTORIC FREDERICKSBURG FOUNDATION, INC., OFFICE AND GIFT SHOP)
1200 Caroline Street

While passing by the Lewis Store in 1943, well-known scholar of Virginia architecture Thomas T. Waterman described the Lewis Store to a friend as "one of the finest and most unique architecturally in this town." Built in the mid-1700s, at the start of the consumer revolution, this unique example of early Georgian-styled commercial architecture survives as one of our nation's oldest urban retail buildings.

Colonel John Lewis II (1694–1754), a prominent shipping merchant in Colonial Fredericksburg, built the store in 1749. Standing one-and-a-half stories tall, the handsome brick building featured carved stone lintels above the doors and windows and prominent quoins at the corners made of Aquia sandstone (a local material quarried in neighboring Stafford County, which was used to build the first sections of the White House and the U.S. Capitol). The main selling room was separated by a narrow storage hall from the counting room

As it stood in the mid-twentieth century, the Lewis Store was in desperate need of maintenance and repair. (Historic Fredericksburg Foundation, Inc.)

The fully restored Lewis Store is now headquarters for the Historic Fredericksburg Foundation, Inc., a local non-profit group advocating for preservation in the Fredericksburg region.

in back. Surplus wares were stored in the basement and on the floor above, accessed by an exterior loading door on the building's front. A specially designed display window installed near the building's southeast corner—the oldest such window for which physical evidence survives—previewed select wares imported from the West Indies, London, Brisbane, and other international ports for a clientele that included, among others, a young George Washington.

Retail operations continued until 1807, when a fire swept through the city's downtown district, damaging the store and scores of other buildings. Ironically, the fire, one of the most destructive in the city's history, had originated in a nearby home once occupied by John Lewis's son, Fielding Lewis (1725–1781), and his family. Rebuilt a year later with a full second story, the Lewis Store continued operating into the early 1820s, when it was finally closed and converted for residential use.

In 1996, the building, then vacant and falling down, was donated by its new owners to the Historic Fredericksburg Foundation, Inc. (HFFI). After a successful decade-long, nearly $1 million restoration effort, the Lewis Store became the Foundation's permanent home in 2006.

www.hffi.org

17

LOWER CAROLINE STREET

Lower Caroline Street—the area below the railroad—was one of the town's first subdivisions, created in the early 1750s by lawyer and speculator Roger Dixon (whose name graces a street in the area). Dixon's efforts to promote the development largely failed. It took decades for the lots to be purchased and improved. Still, lower Caroline is home to some of the oldest, most elegant homes in Fredericksburg.

Ten houses on lower Caroline date to the eighteenth century—by far the largest concentration of such houses in town. Future president James Monroe rented 301 for four years in the 1780s. A few doors down is 213, the oldest house on the street, built in 1764 and commonly associated with one of its more prominent owners, Dr. Charles Mortimer, who was physician to Mary Washington and the town's first mayor. Across the street is 214, home, prior to the Civil War, to the Minor/Blackford family, whose five sons fought for the Confederacy despite their parents' fervent disapproval of slavery. Commodore Matthew Fontaine Maury, a Spotsylvania native whose statue is among the array of Confederate heroes on Richmond's Monument Avenue, also lived here at the outset of the Civil War. (His daughter, Betty, kept a vivid diary of the time.)

The circa 1786 "Sentry Box" on Lower Caroline Street. This was the home of Revolutionary General George Weedon. The house stands in what has been one of Fredericksburg's most prosperous neighborhoods for more than two hundred years.

Several antebellum duplex dwellings line the street, many of which were heavily damaged during the Civil War but painstakingly brought back to life by postwar owners.

A beautiful neighborhood, Lower Caroline is idealistic of historic towns with well-manicured lawns and fine houses.

The Civil War brought great devastation to the homes on lower Caroline. The townhouses at 130–138 appear ravaged in period photographs. Across the street, the "Sentry Box" (133 Caroline) was rendered a virtual skeleton by wartime shelling and looting; today it is widely considered to be one of the most beautiful timber-framed homes in town. After the war, several impressive Victorian-era homes were added to the mix of older structures on Caroline Street. Today, lower Caroline is one of the most picturesque residential streets in Virginia.

18

THE MARY WASHINGTON HOUSE
1200 Charles Street

This frame dwelling was the residence of Mary Ball Washington, the "Mother of the Father of Our Country," from 1772 until her death in 1789. In 1738, Augustine and Mary Washington, together with their five children, moved to a farm situated directly across the river from the town of Fredericksburg. (Simply referred to as "the Washington farm" during the family's tenure, it is known today as "Ferry Farm.") In 1743, Augustine died, leaving Mary a widow at age thirty-five and responsible for raising her children and managing the farm. Three decades later, she was sixty-four and living alone. Seeking to move his mother into the town and away from the isolation and burdens of the family farm, George Washington purchased two adjacent lots on Charles Street in 1771, each of which already contained a small residence. He hired a carpenter who spent one year building a connecting structure between the two existing buildings, leaving the three different and distinct rooflines seen today.

Mary's home stood on one acre of ground and had at least three dependencies. When she moved to the property, she brought two horses, one cow, one dog, and six servants with her, and remained here until her death on August 25,

Living near her daughter, Betty, Mary often walked to Betty's home Kenmore for visits. An arbor located in the rear gardens of Mary Washington House marks the path used to travel between the homes. (Library of Congress)

1789. Shortly before she died, George had visited her to receive her blessings before his inauguration as the country's first president.

In the rear of the property, there is an English-styled garden, recreated by the Garden Club of Virginia in 1969. The original kitchen dependency still stands amid some of the original boxwoods planted by Mary Washington.

Prior to the Civil War, Fredericksburg might have been most famous as the home of Mary Ball Washington, George Washington's mother. Her house still stands on Charles Street.

In 1890, the house was on the verge of being dismantled and taken to Chicago for the upcoming "Columbian Exposition" or "World's Fair." Concerned local citizens arranged for the house to be bought and preserved by the Association for the Preservation of Virginia Antiquities, today known as Preservation Virginia. Washington Heritage Museums took over operation of the museum in 2013.

http://www.washingtonheritagemuseums.org/

19

MARY WASHINGTON MONUMENT

Throughout the 1770s and 1780s, Mary Washington, mother of George, loved walking the gardens around her daughter Betty's home, now known as Kenmore. Her favorite spot was "Meditation Rock"—a natural outcropping located along the northwestern boundary of the Lewis estate. Upon her death in 1789 at the age of eighty-one, Mary was buried at this site at her request.

In a colorful ceremony in 1833, President Andrew Jackson laid the cornerstone of a monument dedicated to Mary near her burial place. More than five thousand people attended the festivities. Unfortunately, the memorial's construction was halted soon after because of a lack of available funds, and the monument remained unfinished for decades.

As plans to develop the surrounding land were under way in the early 1890s, efforts began to complete the unfinished and damaged Mary Washington Monument. The newly established Mary Washington Memorial Association, with local and national chapters, championed building a more imposing monument and creating a wide, double avenue with a center green leading to the gravesite a landscape befitting the memory of Mary Washington and nearby Kenmore

The grave of Mary Washington. The site has been cause for at least four presidential visits to Fredericksburg. President Grover Cleveland dedicated the present memorial in 1894.

mansion. Local landowners donated portions of their lots for the project, and a national campaign appealed to women, particularly those named Mary, to donate to the cause. The money flowed in. Descendants of Mary Washington were part of a record crowd that turned out on May 10, 1894, to watch President Grover Cleveland unveil the new, completed monument. The forty-foot-tall granite obelisk was the first monument ever erected to a woman by women.

President Andrew Jackson dedicated the cornerstone of the memorial in 1833, but fundraising lagged. By the time of the Civil War, the unfinished memorial was nearly a ruin, pocked by the bullets of boys who used it for target practice. (Library of Congress)

In 1896, the Memorial Association arranged for the construction of a small lodge on an adjoining parcel to house both a museum and the monument's caretaker. Behind the monument, a brick-walled cemetery contains the graves of Samuel Gordon and members of his family. He bought the Lewis mansion in 1819 and named it Kenmore, after "Kenmuir," the Gordon family estate in Scotland. The Gordon family lived there for forty years.

20

MASONIC CEMETERY
900 Charles Street

The Masonic Burial Ground, Fredericksburg's second-oldest cemetery, was developed on land donated to the local Masonic Lodge in 1784 by James Somerville, a Scottish merchant and early Fredericksburg mayor.

Many well-known people are buried here, including Lewis Littlepage, who had a distinguished and colorful career as a scholar, diplomat, and soldier, and Basil Gordon and Charles Yates, prominent late-eighteenth century merchants. Also buried here are two early mayors of Fredericksburg: Robert Lewis (son of Fielding Lewis) and Benjamin Day.

Among the impressive crypts is that of General John Minor. While serving in the Virginia House of Delegates, he introduced an unsuccessful bill for the emancipation of slaves in the early nineteenth century. His family was very active in the American Colonization Society, helping ex-slaves who wished to relocate to the African colony that is now the nation of Liberia.

Founded in 1784, the Masonic Cemetery is the burial place for many of Fredericksburg's early leaders, including Revolutionary General George Weedon.

Associated with Fredericksburg's Masonic Lodge No. 4—to which George Washington belonged—this cemetery features some elaborate mortuary art. Washington's nephew Robert Lewis is buried here. (Library of Congress)

Also buried here is Mrs. Christiana Campbell, who operated a successful tavern bearing her name in Williamsburg that was frequented by George Washington and other Colonial leaders. She moved to Fredericksburg in her old age and died here in 1792.

An archaeological dig conducted in 1992 by Mary Washington College (now the University of Mary Washington) determined that the surrounding Aquia sandstone wall was added later.

21
MASONIC LODGE NO. 4
803 Princess Anne Street

The Fredericksburg Masonic Lodge claims to be one of the most historic Lodges in the United States. Established in the first half of the eighteenth century, the Fredericksburg Masonic Lodge has the distinction of being the Mother Lodge of George Washington, who became a member on November 4, 1752. The current Lodge building was constructed in the early nineteenth century. In 1813, the Male Charity School started construction of a new schoolhouse at 803 Princess Anne. A lack of funding halted construction, resulting in a search for financial investors. As luck would have it, the Fredericksburg Masonic Lodge was seeking a permanent home. With assistance from the Masons, the school building was completed in 1816, with an agreement that the Masons receive full use of the third floor. In 1824, during a visit to the United States, the Marquis de Lafayette became an honorary member of the Lodge.

The Male Charity School and Masonic Lodge coexisted in the building until 1867 when the Male Charity School and the Female Charity School merged. The combined school was housed in a new building behind the extant brick structure. In 1910, the Masonic Lodge bought all buildings on the parcel from

The current home of Masonic Lodge No. 4 dates to 1816, but the organization is much older. George Washington belonged to this Lodge, as did many of Fredericksburg's most prominent citizens.

The building's façade went through many changes over the years until 1952 when the Lodge restored the front to its original as part of a celebration for George Washington becoming a member two hundred years prior. (Library of Congress)

the Charity School for $5,000. Prior to the sale, expanding the front and adding a Victorian-styled castellated tower enlarged the brick building. As part of the 1952 bicentennial celebration honoring George Washington's association with the Masons, the Fredericksburg Masonic Lodge restored the front of the building and added a brick wing to the back—as seen today.

Over the years, the Masonic Lodge has participated in many ceremonies related to its rich history, including laying cornerstones for the Mary Washington Monument, the Washington Monument in the District of Columbia, and the George Washington Masonic National Memorial in Alexandria, Virginia. As in many communities, the Masons have assisted in the establishment of many buildings in Fredericksburg, seen on cornerstones throughout the city. While proud of its past, the Lodge continues to make history through its constant contributions to the community. The Bible used by George Washington as he took his Masonic oath, a punch bowl used by Lafayette at the time of his reception in the 1820s, and other Masonic artifacts, including two Gilbert Stuart portraits of George Washington, are now housed at the Fredericksburg Area Museum. The Lodge still uses the Bible for ceremonial occasions.

www.masoniclodge4.com

22

NATIONAL BANK OF VIRGINIA
900 Princess Anne Street

The Farmers Bank of Virginia, which first opened in Fredericksburg in 1812, erected the building at 900 Princess Anne in 1820. A side entrance led to the residence of the bank's cashiers, who lived in the back and on the second floor.

Prior to the Civil War, the Taliaferro family occupied the upstairs. We know about this period through a remarkable memoir written by John Washington, a slave owned by the mistress of the household, Catherine Taliaferro. John was born in 1838. His mother Sarah cooked for the Taliaferro family until they hired her and her other children out to a farm in Staunton. Beginning at the tender age of eleven, John alone remained with the Taliaferro family in the bank building until the occupation of Fredericksburg by Union troops in 1862, when he escaped across the Rappahannock River to freedom and joined the main body of the Union Army as camp laborer and aide.

In 1862, during the Union forces' occupation, General Marsena Patrick, the military governor, used the building as his headquarters. In May 1862,

Postcard of the Kitchen dependency. Relocated to Route 1 in the 1950s, this building originally served as the kitchen for the Farmer's Bank building on Princess Anne Street. Sarah, the mother of the slave John Washington, likely worked in this building. (Bill Garner)

Built as a bank and still used as a financial institution, this building also housed the bank's manager in its early days. Before the Civil War, the slave John Washington lived in this building. His memoir of slavery is a vivid testimony to a life striving toward freedom.

President Lincoln, accompanied by Secretary of War Stanton, crossed the Rappahannock on one of the temporary pontoon bridges to address soldiers and citizens from the steps of this bank. Although many buildings around the bank were heavily damaged or destroyed during the Battle of Fredericksburg in December 1862, it suffered comparatively minor damage when cannonballs struck the roof and rear pediment. Despite the survival of the building, the bank's assets, primarily in Confederate notes and bonds, were worthless in 1865, resulting in acquisition of the bank by the directors of the newly founded National Bank of Fredericksburg.

In 1982, a major restoration was undertaken of both the exterior and interior of the bank building to emulate its pre–Civil War appearance. Distinguished by its quintessential Federal-style architecture, including a pedimented temple facade, the National Bank, now a National Historic Landmark and a Virginia State Landmark, houses a museum exhibit in its rear lobby about the history of banking in Fredericksburg. After nearly two hundred years, the bank continues to operate today as a branch of PNC.

http://www.pnclegacyproject.com/banks/fredericksburg.html

23

PLANTER'S HOTEL AND THE SLAVE AUCTION BLOCK

Few people recognize the building on the northwest corner of Charles and William streets for what it is: the oldest standing hotel in Fredericksburg, the Planter's. Noted Spotsylvania hotelier and prominent local businessman Joseph Sanford constructed the hotel, which dates to about 1840. Sanford held the building until 1852, allowing it to run down considerably. By the eve of the Civil War, Planter's had passed to hotelier Counselor Cole. Freedman Nathan Odle, a well-known barber, used the basement.

The ambitions that Cole had for Planter's fell victim to the Civil War. While Southerners maintained control of the town, Cole rented rooms and his brick stable to the Confederates. (The stable still stands to the north of the hotel.) During the Union occupation in 1862, Planter's was apparently the only hotel in town that remained open, though coming battles changed that.

Like many large Fredericksburg buildings, the hotel became a hospital during the war. As the Battles of the Wilderness and Spotsylvania raged in 1864, the Union Army quartered 250 wounded soldiers of the Ninth Corps in Planter's.

Planter's Hotel, built in the 1840s, served as a field hospital during the Civil War and is one of just four buildings in town known to have been visited by Clara Barton, founder of the American Red Cross. Inset: Slave auction block. Likely installed as a carriage step, the block in front of the Planter's Hotel became known for its associations with the auction of enslaved individuals and personal property.

At least six auctions of slaves are known to have taken place on the corner of Charles and William Streets. Several former slaves recalled being sold from the block, including Albert Crutchfield, shown here in this early-twentieth century postcard. (Historic Fredericksburg Foundation, Inc.)

The hotel is one of only four of buildings in Fredericksburg confirmed to have been visited by Clara Barton during her various visits and ministrations in town. After the war, R. T. Knox & Sons purchased the hotel and converted it to offices and a salesroom. It became known as the Knoxanna Building.

On the street corner in front of the hotel stands one of the most compelling urban artifacts in the United States. The sandstone block was likely created as a carriage step but became known as an auction block. On this corner, auctioneers sold all types of goods, including enslaved African Americans. At least five slave sales here in the 1850s and early 1860s are documented, and many more likely took place. In the wake of one of the more successful sales, a local newspaper proclaimed, "Fredericksburg seems to be the best place to sell slaves in the State."

24

PRINCESS ANNE STREET

Visitors sometimes miss Princess Anne Street, for there are few shops on its historic length. But to Fredericksburgers, Princess Anne Street is the cultural and political heart of the community, and it has been since the town's founding in 1728.

Sitting on the ridge three blocks from the river, Princess Anne is home to the town's familiar skyline—a vista made famous in dozens of historic images. The steeples of Fredericksburg Baptist Church and St. George's Episcopal Church dominate the upper part of town from their perches on the east side of the street. (The town clock on St. George's steeple was a convenient target for Union cannoneers during the Civil War.) Nearby are three other church build-ings—the Presbyterian Church, old St. Mary's Catholic Church (built in 1858 and now adapted for offices), and Shiloh Baptist Church (New Site)—that render Princess Anne Street an unmatched corridor of religiosity.

Government was, and still is, a prominent part of the streetscape. Two doors south of the Episcopal Church is James Renwick's Gothic Revival–styled Circuit

Princess Anne Street, once the cultural center of town. Masonic Lodge No. 4 is at right, with the rounded cupola of the Courthouse and steeple of St. George's Episcopal Church in the distance.

Courthouse, which was built in 1852 and is likely the most distinctive building in town with its cupola. Town Hall was on Princess Anne for 170 years—today the building is part of the Fredericksburg Area Museum—and City Hall now occupies the old post office at the corner of Hanover Street. One of the oldest continuously used bank buildings in Virginia sits at the

With the exception of horse stables to the right and an unpaved road, little has changed along this section of Princess Anne Street. (Library of Congress)

corner of George Street, the National Bank of Fredericksburg/PNC Bank. Abraham Lincoln visited this building in 1862; the slave John Washington also grew up in the residence within the bank. His recently published diary provides an eloquent description of life in prewar Fredericksburg for enslaved individuals.

Prior to the Civil War, upper Princess Anne Street was home to some of Fredericksburg's most powerful and prosperous residents. The four corners of the intersection of Lewis and Princess Anne constitute a seat of residential power witnessed in few other areas of the city. Although now subsumed within the core of historic downtown, these residences provide the perfect capstone for this notable city corridor.

RISING SUN TAVERN
1304 Caroline Street

Although the establishment lost its food and liquor licenses over a hundred years ago, the Rising Sun Tavern has remained one of the community's most notable local landmarks. The central part of this structure was originally built in 1762 as a residence for Charles Washington, brother of George Washington. After twenty years, Charles left Fredericksburg and moved to western Virginia to establish a new life near what is today Charles Town, West Virginia.

Leased by John Frazier in 1792 and converted to a tavern, the site served that function for many years as The Eagle and later The Golden Eagle. By 1823, the establishment was known as Rising Sun Tavern, but by 1830, the building was once again a private residence and later a boarding house.

Owned by Preservation Virginia (formerly the Association for the Preservation of Virginia Antiquities [APVA]) for decades, the building was restored as an eighteenth-century tavern. During the restoration process, sections of the old bar were discovered and assembled in the taproom, which contains a remarkable collection

This late-eighteenth century building once housed a vibrant tavern that catered to a host of visitors to Fredericksburg. The front porch was added in the mid-twentieth century to restore the building to its Colonial appearance.

The tavern prior to restoration exhibiting its nineteenth-century portico over the front door. (Library of Congress)

of early pewter. The iconic front porch, removed in the early twentieth century, was reconstructed in mid-century under the guidance of the APVA, which was able to provide architectural and archival evidence of the building's historic appearance.

Visitors can experience life at an "upper tavern," where well-heeled guests slept only three or four to each bed—in contrast with the "lower taverns" near Sophia Street and the river, where customers (usually sailors) were subject to less formal rules.

Today, the tavern is owned and operated by Washington Heritage Museums, who continue to care for the collection and provide guests with a unique view of Fredericksburg's Colonial-era social life.

http://www.washingtonheritagemuseums.org/

26

SHILOH BAPTIST CHURCH (NEW SITE)
525 Princess Anne Street

In June 1886, the rear wall of Shiloh Baptist Church on Sophia Street collapsed after sustaining notable flood damage. Because the building was unsafe for services, the congregation gained permission to meet in the City Courthouse. This arrangement continued for approximately one year as members worked to establish another permanent structure for worship.

While still worshipping at the temporary site, the congregation purchased land for a new church at the corner of Princess Anne and Wolfe Streets. This created a great divide between the parishioners because some members sought to rebuild the church on Sophia Street, while others wanted to move away from the flood zone. The disagreement led to a physical and metaphorical split in the congregation, some opting to stay at the old site while others started a new church.

Members of the new church congregation continued to meet at the Courthouse while raising funds for a permanent church. On June 9, 1890, a cornerstone was laid on the new plot of land, marking the beginning of

Although the building footprint expanded over the years to accommodate a growing congregation, the late-nineteenth-century façade of Shiloh Baptist Church (New Site) still retains its original architectural decorative elements.

The importance of the history of this African-American congregation is attested through its inclusion in a 1908 book on the history of Fredericksburg, just eighteen years after the church was built. (*The History of the City of Fredericksburg, Virginia* by S. J. Quinn, 1908)

construction of an Italianate-styled church.

Another argument arose among the members of the now-divided Shiloh Baptist Church regarding who had the right to the name "Shiloh." The argument was eventually settled in court. Judge William S. Barton appeased both congregations when he ruled that both churches could use the designation Shiloh Baptist Church—however, the Sophia Street church would be designated "Old Site" and the Princess Anne Street church as "New Site."

Shiloh (New Site) became the cornerstone of a new African American neighborhood at the corner of Princess Anne and Wolfe Streets in the early twentieth century, which included a school (on the site now occupied by the Fire Station), houses, and stores. Today, the church and a few dwellings on Wolfe Street are the only physical reminders of this enclave.

http://www.angelfire.com/va/firstshirt/

27

SHILOH BAPTIST CHURCH (OLD SITE)
801 Sophia Street

Shiloh Baptist Church (Old Site) originated with the formation of the Fredericksburg Baptist Church in 1818. In the mid-nineteenth century, racial tensions within the Fredericksburg Baptist Church grew, and as a result, the church split on May 4, 1856. The white congregation moved to 1019 Princess Anne Street, while the black congregation remained in the Sophia Street church. The Sophia Street location, then called the African Baptist Church of Fredericksburg, flourished.

At the time, Virginia law did not allow black congregations to be led by black ministers, so the Reverend George Rowe, a plantation owner, oversaw the preaching. He remained in this position until 1863, when the Emancipation Proclamation made it legal for black congregations to have black preachers. The first African American pastor at Shiloh was the Reverend George Dixon.

On the eve of the Civil War, racial tensions rose, and most members of Shiloh fled. Some moved to the surrounding counties, holding meetings at various locations. Other members crossed the Rappahannock River to escape from the South and found safety in Washington, D.C. While in the federal capital, members formed a new Shiloh Baptist Church, still in existence today, with one of the largest congregations in the District of Columbia. Among the fleeing members was John Washington, a slave who, after the war, authored a now-famous memoir detailing his escape from Fredericksburg during the hostilities.

Shiloh Baptist Church (Old Site) constructed the present building, shown here, in the 1880s. The original congregation spawned two other churches in downtown Fredericksburg.

Most members of Shiloh in Fredericksburg reunited after the war and started to repair their church. In June 1886, floods hit the city, resulting in the collapse of the building's rear wall. The church began rebuilding on June 18, 1890. However, soon after, the church split once again. The

Shiloh Baptist Church (Old Site) was born as the African Baptist Church just before the Civil War. It remains the oldest historically African-American church in Fredericksburg. (Shiloh Baptist Church [Old Site] Archives)

congregation is still active today, and the building is a social and physical anchor on an ever-changing Sophia Street landscape.

http://www.shiloholdsite.org/

28
SOPHIA STREET

Every town has a street or neighborhood that is home to all of those buildings and businesses that do not seem to fit elsewhere—the place where constant change is the rule and constancy seems elusive. Fredericksburg's Sophia Street is such a place. Known for decades as Water Street, its status as Fredericksburg's "utility room" is rooted in its nearness to the river, which every few years rose to submerge sections of the street, rendering all in its path damaged, if not ruined. The regular ebb and flow of water, along with every town's need for utility space, rendered Sophia Street what it was: a slightly awkward, sporadic mix of open space, modest houses, and tenements, with a sprinkling of warehouses, outhouses, and even a jail thrown in.

The community icehouse was here for many years, sitting incongruously next to what was at first called the African Baptist Church and is today known as Shiloh Baptist Church (Old Site). Below the church was a mix of tenements and single-family homes, steadily demolished over the years, mostly to make way for new parking in the twentieth century. At the end of the Chatham Bridge stands the Old Stone Warehouse—the only building in town built in

Built in 1813, the old stone warehouse at the west of the Chatham Bridge is the type of utilitarian building that once was common on the Rappahannock riverfront.

Though little has changed on the building itself since the 1920s, the surrounding topography has been greatly altered, including raising the road grade to allow the formation of a neighboring intersection and bridge, thus burying the original first story underground. (Library of Congress)

response to war (not the Civil War, but the threat from the British posed during the War of 1812).

Above Chatham Bridge, where flooding was not a problem, Sophia Street has had a more settled existence. Historically, the river side of the street was dotted with a few small industries and homes. The town side has, for two centuries, been a residential neighborhood. This section of Sophia Street was badly damaged during the Union bombardment of December 11, 1862. Indeed, along its entire length, just nine antebellum buildings still stand on Sophia Street.

The twentieth century has brought more change: as Fredericksburg morphed from a riverine community to a road-based society, Sophia Street was no longer integral to the town's economic well-being. Despite a gradual decline in population and architectural integrity during the twentieth century, the area is now experiencing a rebirth as the city reestablishes its connection to the geographic feature that gave it life.

In 1862, with no bridges to cross, Union soldiers constructed several pontoon bridges across the Rappahannock River. The bridges allowed Union troops to storm the City of Fredericksburg in an offensive attack of Confederate forces.

29

ST. GEORGE'S EPISCOPAL CHURCH AND GRAVEYARD
905 Princess Anne Street

The present St. George's Church is the third church built on this site. In 1728, when Fredericksburg was created by the General Assembly, two lots were set aside for the established church of Colonial Virginia, the Church of England. St. George's Church was a part of St. George's Parish, which was created in 1720 to include newly formed Spotsylvania County. After the Revolutionary War, the Colonial Anglican Church was reorganized into the Protestant Episcopal Church in the United States of America.

The current building was completed in 1849, crafted in the Gothic Revival style with Romanesque Revival influences. It was designed and built by Robert Cary Long and H. R. Reynold of Baltimore. The trio of arched exterior doors and the tower with its steeple and clock are visually iconic markers of the Gothic Revival style, while the interior follows the ancient basilica plan with a nave and columns that form a court on three sides and support the galleries. The original church windows of clear, diamond-shaped glass panes were replaced with stained glass. Noteworthy are the three Tiffany windows and

St. George's houses the oldest congregation in the city, dating to 1732. The present sanctuary was built in 1849; the town clock still keeps time.

a window in memory of Mary Ball Washington, mother of George Washington.

During the Civil War, the church was badly damaged. Its steeple and clock were favorite targets for the Union cannoneers situated on Stafford Heights. It served as a hospital during the Battles of Fredericksburg and the Wilderness. Religious revival meetings were held in the building for the Confederate troops during

Owing to its location at a prominent intersection and the majestic height of its steeple, the church has been a focal point for residents and visitors for centuries. (Library of Congress)

The cemetery found adjacent to the church is the final resting place of many of Fredericksburg's earliest citizens.

1863. The silver communion set was stolen in 1862 but recovered piece by piece over seventy years.

Despite these catastrophes, the church was rebuilt and the congregation continued to grow throughout the twentieth century. In 2009, the choir and organ were restored to their original location in the rear gallery.

The St. George's graveyard dates back to the first church, which was built in 1735. The oldest existing tombstone, dating to 1752, marks the grave of John Jones, one of Fredericksburg's early tavern keepers. Martha Washington's father, Colonel John Dandridge, is also buried here, as is William Paul, brother of John Paul Jones. During renovation of adjoining Market Square in 2001, eighteenth-century skeletal remains of three men, two women, and one teenage boy were unearthed. The following year, on All Saints Day, the remains were reinterred in St. George's Cemetery. The brick building to the left of the cemetery was constructed in 1823 and was used as a Sunday school for enslaved African American children before the war.

http://www.stgeorgesepiscopal.net/

30

THE ST. JAMES HOUSE
1300 Charles Street

The St. James House is at the edge of the designated Historic District and is one of the few eighteenth-century frame homes still standing in this area. Built in 1768 by a prominent local lawyer, James Mercer, the house can be described as a "gentleman's cottage," but, in fact, is quite small. He named his estate "St. James" in honor of the Dublin, Ireland, street on which his family's old house had stood.

Mercer played an active role in civic affairs. He was one of Virginia's delegates to the Continental Congress in 1779 and a member of the new state's first Executive Council. After the Revolutionary War, he became the first president of the Fredericksburg Academy, a school that occupied the grounds of the then-defunct Fredericksburg Gun Manufactory. Mercer ended his career serving as a judge on the Virginia Court of Appeals in Richmond.

The St. James House later became the home of the Howison family and the childhood home of noted Civil War diarist Jane Howison Beale. Privately

The Dutch Colonial-styled dwelling at the intersection of Charles and Fauquier Streets is emblematic of the small, early residential buildings that once lined the city's streets.

restored in 1963, the house contains a collection of eighteenth-century porcelain, glass, and furniture. St. James is one of four Fredericksburg properties owned and administered by Washington Heritage Museums. The house is open to the public only two weeks a year: the third week of April (during springtime's Virginia Garden Week) and the first full week of October.

Like its exterior, the interior rooms of the St. James House still resemble their Colonial appearance, including original mantles and moldings. (Washington Heritage Museums)

http://www.washingtonheritagemuseums.org/

31

SUNKEN ROAD AND MARYE'S HEIGHTS
Between Hanover Street and Lafayette Boulevard

In Fredericksburg, the Civil War remains the central event in the town's history and identity, and it is from the Sunken Road that that history speaks most vividly.

For 130 years, it was a road like thousands of others in America. First called the Courthouse Road, then Telegraph Road, it carried wagons into Fredericksburg from surrounding farms, or townsfolk from the town to visit relatives in the country, or even an odd world traveler or two exploring a still relatively new nation. But on December 13, 1862, the road shed its former names and became simply the "Sunken Road." It emerged as one of the most famous byways in America. To this day, anyone interested in the Civil War will know the place. The Sunken Road. Fredericksburg. Union disaster. All are inextricably linked.

On December 13, 1862, waves of Union soldiers—thirty thousand men—swept toward the Confederate line in the Sunken Road. The Confederates, protected

The stone walls that bordered the Sunken Road made nearly perfect cover for Confederate soldiers firing on the thousands of Union soldiers who tried, but failed, to reach the road on December 13, 1862.

by the stone wall bordering the road, fired into the Union masses as fast as they could. "Each one of us fired over one hundred rounds," wrote one North Carolinian. "Our shoulders were kicked blue from the muskets and were sore for many days."

For seven hours, the fighting raged. One thousand Union soldiers fell each hour—most of them in what is today a three-block section of Fredericksburg. The Confederates lost one-eighth that number. It was a Union disaster on a scale unmatched, and its impact reverberated through parlors, churches, and even Congress for months to come.

What is today known as the Innis House was brand-new at the time of the Civil War, but suffered severely in the 1862 battle. Its interior walls bear as much visible battle damage as probably any house in America.

The memorial to Confederate Sergeant Richard Kirkland, who according to legend, left the Sunken Road to aid wounded Union soldiers on the plain in front.

After that bloody day, the newly christened "Sunken Road" returned to its pre-war languid state, and over time—as the town of Fredericksburg grew into a city—the road became a typical city street. In 2005, the National Park Service restored it to its 1862 appearance.

http://www.nps.gov/frsp

The graves of thousands of Union soldiers can be found on the hilly landscape of the National Cemetery. Most of the individuals buried here are unidentified, known only by the numbers they were assigned when interred in the cemetery after the war.

32

THOMAS JEFFERSON
RELIGIOUS FREEDOM MONUMENT

The Thomas Jefferson Religious Freedom Monument commemorates Thomas Jefferson's drafting of the Virginia Statute for Religious Freedom here in Fredericksburg. Jefferson served as chairman of a committee tasked with making revisions of Colonial laws, which met at Weedon's Tavern on Caroline Street in January 1777. The other committee members were George Mason, George Wythe, Edmund Pendleton, and Thomas Ludwell Lee.

While the group worked on the body of laws, Jefferson established and authored the essence of what became the Virginia Statute for Religious Freedom. The document was adopted virtually unchanged by the Virginia General Assembly on December 16, 1785. It established the principle that "no man shall suffer on account of his religious opinions and beliefs."

The Virginia Statute inspired the First Amendment to the United States Constitution, which was incorporated into the Bill of Rights in 1789. Jefferson regarded the document on the separation of church and state as one of the

major accomplishments of his life. In fact, on his self-designed tombstone, he had written: "Here was buried Thomas Jefferson/Author of the Declaration of American Independence/of the Virginia Statue of Religious Freedom/ and Father of the University of Virginia." There is no mention of his presidential tenure.

This simple but majestic stone monument commemorates one of the most important early documents in American history, authored in Fredericksburg.

The monument was unveiled at the two hundredth anniversary of George Washington's birth on October 16, 1932, at its original location near Maury School on Barton Street. It was moved to its present site on Washington Avenue and rededicated on January 13, 1977. An annual multidenominational religious service is held at the monument to celebrate America's commitment to religious freedom.

Jefferson's document on religious freedom was authored at a downtown Fredericksburg tavern operated by General George Weedon. Although demolished in the nineteenth century, records suggest that the building was a simple, wood-framed structure that housed all of the required amenities for early travelers, including warm fires, good food, and sturdy stables. (*Forgotten Companions* by Paula Felder, 1982)

33

THORNTON'S TAVERN/HUNTER'S STORE
523 Sophia Street

Most people just walk by this unassuming house. It is not very large. It has no unique decoration. And it seems, well, ordinary. But this small dwelling at the foot of Wolfe Street may, in fact, be the oldest building in Fredericksburg. In 1737, Henry Willis, one of the richest men in town, petitioned the County Court to operate a ferry and an ordinary on this property. The business, managed by Thomas Thornton, was known as Thornton's Tavern. The stone foundation still visible today is part of the tavern. The ferry lane ran to the north of the building, and the structure was originally designed to face north onto the lane. William Hunter constructed the extant building on the stone tavern foundation in 1746. He and his nephew, James, ran a mercantile shop out of this structure for thirty years.

The building became a private residence in the nineteenth century. One notable resident was Elizabeth Long Eubanks. Not only did she own property in an age when few women were landholders, but also she was instrumental in the revival of the colonial ferry during the Civil War, once again needed after the area bridges had been burned.

Constructed in 1746, this is one of the oldest standing buildings in Fredericksburg. Note its location at the foot of Wolfe Street, offset from the prominent surrounding street grid, because it was built before the street system was firmly established throughout town.

By the time this photo was taken in 1937, what was once a tavern had been in use as a residence for 150 years. (Library of Virginia)

The house itself was significantly damaged by fire in about 1890. While repairs were made, the main entry was relocated from the north side, facing the ferry road, to the west side, fronting Sophia Street. This move is emblematic of the larger shift in town planning, which reflected the changing emphasis from the river to the roads and rail. Although hidden under modern materials, this building retains many characteristics of its earliest days as a tavern and mercantile shop.

34

TOWN HALL/MARKET HOUSE
907 Princess Anne Street

Frederickburg's historic Town Hall/Market House is a vivid reminder of the town's English roots. The central marketplace, surrounded by the center of government, official buildings, and a dominant church, bespeaks Fredericksburg's founding in 1728. For 250 years, the town's government was located here. Until the early twentieth century, merchants sold their goods—everything from nails to fish and (probably) slaves—in the open-air stalls beneath the Town Hall and in the adjacent market, now known as Market Square.

Dominating the landscape today is the Town Hall/Market House, built in 1816 and, until 1982, the seat of Fredericksburg's government. (The first Town Hall stood along the Caroline Street side of the Square from 1765 to 1814.) Here, the mayor and Town Council kept the town running, passing laws controlling the passage of pigs through the streets, directing investment of town funds into railroads and a canal, creating ordinances governing the behavior of slaves and free blacks on the streets of Fredericksburg, and even negotiating with Union authorities for the town's peaceful surrender in 1862. Town Hall also included meeting space and,

The 1816 town hall was home to Fredericksburg's government or more than 150 years. The building also included rooms used for community functions and even a church. (Library of Congress)

at various times, housed a library, newspaper publisher, and a nascent church.

In 1824, Town Hall hosted one of the greatest social events in Fredericksburg's history when Revolutionary War hero Marquis de Lafayette visited Fredericksburg during his American tour. War touched the place more ominously in the 1860s. Confederate General William Barksdale used Town Hall and the adjacent Square as his headquarters during the vicious street fighting in town on December 11, 1862. Later, the building was turned into a hospital for wounded Union soldiers at three different times.

Town Hall is still owned by the City of Fredericksburg, but today is home to the Fredericksburg Area Museum and Cultural Center. Using both Town Hall and the historic Planters Bank building across the street, the museum houses permanent exhibitions and changing galleries that interpret the culture and history of the region across centuries—local history that tells a national story.

www.famcc.org

Fredericksburg Town Hall is an excellent example of the Federal style for architecture, a popular format in the late-eighteenth and early-nineteenth century that celebrated America's early Federal governmental system and the beauty of simplicity in design.

The stalls of the old marketplace that once operated from the lowest level of Town Hall are still visible. Today, the building is part of the Fredericksburg Area Museum complex.

35

UNIVERSITY OF MARY WASHINGTON
1301 College Avenue

Established in 1908 as Fredericksburg Normal and Industrial School for Women, the University of Mary Washington (UMW) is today a vibrant, coeducational, liberal arts school that is part of the college/university system of the Commonwealth of Virginia. In the 1920s, the institution was renamed Fredericksburg State Teachers College, providing education, training, and degrees for women seeking licensure as teachers. In 1944, it became the Mary Washington College of the University of Virginia, the women's branch of that school, which was then all male. The college became coed in 1970 and a completely independent state entity of higher education in 1972. In 2004, the college achieved university status and altered its name accordingly.

The main campus, located in the City of Fredericksburg, is the undergraduate center of the university and has just over four thousand students enrolled in thirty-five programs. In addition, the growing graduate campus, in neighboring Stafford County, has one thousand students and offers four advanced-degree programs.

Virginia Hall, built in 1915. Flanking both sides of Monroe Hall are two residential halls with a unique H-shaped footprint.

Constructed in 1911, Monroe Hall was the first academic and administrative building on campus.

With green spaces, Jefferson-influenced architecture, and superb landscaping, the University of Mary Washington presents students with an inviting campus experience.

The buildings of the original campus are still at the center of the Fredericksburg neighborhood known as College Heights. Many lectures and events are sponsored for the campus and local community throughout the year, offering Fredericksburg-area residents a broad selection of activities, as well as educational and cultural programs. Because of its location within the boundaries of historic Marye's Heights, there are a number of Civil War sites within the campus boundaries; these sites can be toured by picking up a self-guided map at the campus center.

www.umw.edu

36

BELMONT/THE GARI MELCHERS HOME AND STUDIO
224 Washington Street, Falmouth, Stafford County

Situated high above the Rappahannock River in Falmouth, Virginia, this late-eighteenth-century frame dwelling is best known for its association with American Naturalist painter Julius Garibaldi "Gari" Melchers (1860–1932). Melchers and his wife, Corrine, purchased the house and twenty-seven acres in 1916.

The original owners of the house and the exact date of its construction are not known, but the style of the dwelling—late Georgian/early Federal—and documentary evidence suggest that the earliest section was built in the 1790s. In 1825, Joseph B. Ficklen, a wealthy mill owner, acquired the property and significantly enlarged the house in the 1840s. By the time Gari and Corrine Melchers bought the property, it was in decline. However, after years of living as expatriates in Europe, they were enchanted with their pastoral retreat and spent years modernizing the house and enhancing the grounds. One distinctive architectural feature that dates to the couple's tenure is a hexagonal sun porch at the south end of the house. They also restored and expanded the formal gardens, adding a stone summerhouse that serves as a landmark to this day.

Gari Melchers enjoyed international acclaim and commercial success in his lifetime—associating with luminaries such as George Hitchcock and John Singer Sargent and receiving commissions to paint portraits of clients with surnames such as Mellon and Roosevelt. After her husband's death in 1932, Corrine Melchers continued to live in the home until her death in 1955. The estate was willed to the Commonwealth of Virginia to help preserve Gari Melchers' legacy.

Though built about 1790, Falmouth's Belmont is most famous for its twentieth-century owner, the artist Gari Melchers. Today, Belmont is operated by the University of Mary Washington as a historic house and art museum.

Wanting a private art studio at his residences, work on the studio began in the early 1920s and was completed in 1924 using local Aquia sandstone. Today the studio houses a large collection of Melchers work.

Although, Gari Melchers' contributions to the world of art have been obscured by the passage of time, visitors to Belmont can witness evidence of his genius—and that of Corrine, who was also an artist—as they wander through the stone studio. In addition, the couple filled their home with an eclectic collection of antique furniture and objets d'art acquired during their years abroad. The home is administered by the University of Mary Washington, which sponsors many community activities there throughout the year.

http://www.umw.edu/gari_melchers/

37

CHATHAM, OR THE "LACY HOUSE"
120 Chatham Lane, Stafford County

Wealthy local planter William Fitzhugh constructed this exquisite and expansive residence in 1768. Fitzhugh was closely involved with the burgeoning patriot movement of the Virginia Colony and supported the Revolutionary struggle as a manager of one of the area's gun works supplying armaments to the Continental Army.

He was a friend of George Washington and entertained him at Chatham, as well as hosting Thomas Jefferson (a cousin of Fitzhugh's wife) during the 1790s. By 1806, Fitzhugh had sold Chatham, leading to a series of subsequent owners. In 1859, the diminished but still vast estate was purchased by J. Horace Lacy, who owned the plantation during the Civil War era when it was called "the Lacy House."

In early 1862, Abraham Lincoln visited the home and held a strategy session with some of his military advisors. At the end of that year, during the Battle of Fredericksburg, the Lacy House became a hospital for Union troops, adding another layer of noted Americans who came here: Clara Barton, Walt

The 185-foot-long home built by William Fitzhugh in 1771 once dominated the view from Fredericksburg to the east. It is the only home in America whose threshold was crossed by both Washington and Lincoln.

This Civil War–era stereoscopic image of Chatham highlights the building's nineteenth-century appearance, including the two-storied porch once located on the building. (Library of Congress)

Whitman, and Dr. Mary Edwards Walker, who became the first woman to be awarded the Medal of Honor.

Overshadowed by these dramatic and noteworthy events were the labor and contributions, almost never acknowledged, of enslaved workers and other servants who made the plantation operable. In one case, there was an insurrection of these workers and, in another, an owner (before the Civil War) tried to free the slaves of Chatham in her will, which lawyers later overturned.

By the end of the nineteenth century, Chatham had fallen into grave disrepair and gone through multiple owners. It was the Devore family who completely renovated and added to the grounds during the 1920s. They hired Ellen Shipman, one of the first women landscape architects, to create a Colonial Revival garden. The last private owner of Chatham, King George native and General Motors executive John Lee Pratt, bought the home and remaining acreage for $150,000 in 1931. Pratt, who died in 1975, bequeathed the estate to the National Park Service, which today uses the site both as a headquarters and a museum.

http://www.nps.gov/frsp/chatham.htm

FERRY FARM
268 King's Highway (Virginia Route 3 East), Stafford County

In 1730, young Mary Ball became the second wife of the recently widowed Augustine Washington, who had purchased the area known as "Ferry Farm" from the estate of William Strother. Together, they moved to the farm in 1738 to more closely manage a local ironworks for a group of English investors. The mid-sized farm and its buildings were typical of the times, reflecting the agrarian economy of Colonial Virginia and attendant lifestyle. Washington's son, George, was six years old at the time and would cross the river amid vessels arriving from, and departing for, European ports so he could be in the streets of the newly established town of Fredericksburg. Upon the death of her husband in 1743, Mary Ball Washington continued to manage the farm herself. She never remarried.

In 1772, when Mary Washington moved into Fredericksburg, the farm was sold to Fredericksburg émigré Hugh Mercer and, eventually, to a succession of other owners. In early 1862, Abraham Lincoln, an admirer of Washington, visited the site as he crossed the river on a visit to the region. During the Battle of Fredericksburg in December 1862, Ferry Farm's strategic location,

The Ferry Farm household was established on a bluff above the Rappahannock River. Occupants, including the Washingtons, took advantage of a natural lane leading to the riverbank as a lane leading to a successful ferry operation.

high above the river offered Union artillery an opportunity both to cover a bridge crossing and to bombard Confederate positions on the opposite bank.

After a succession of owners in the late-nineteenth and twentieth centuries, Ferry Farm's importance and connection with the Washington story were forgotten, and the physical landscape was obscured by development. Acquired by the Kenmore Association (now the George Washington Foundation) in 1996, Ferry Farm is once again bustling, but now with archaeologists seeking to discover information the Washingtons left behind, hidden for hundreds of years.

http://kenmore.org/

The discovery of the original foundations of the house of Washington's youth made national news in 2008. This is the legendary site of the cherry tree and the literal home of Washington for most of his childhood. (George Washington Foundation)

39

BATTLEFIELDS BEYOND FREDERICKSBURG
Spotsylvania and Orange Counties

For a period of eighteen months spanning the years 1862, 1863, and 1864, armies camped, maneuvered, and fought upon the landscape around Fredericksburg. Four major battles rendered the land here the bloodiest in North America. More than that, what happened here both reflected and affected the ebb and flow of America's Civil War.

In May 1863, Confederate General Robert E. Lee won what many consider to be his greatest victory at Chancellorsville. Success there opened the way for a raid into the North—a movement that came to a climax at Gettysburg. But the victory at Chancellorsville came at heavy cost. Stonewall Jackson fell mortally wounded by his own men. He died on May 10, 1863, a day of catastrophe for the Confederate nation.

A year later, a few miles west of Chancellorsville, the armies collided again. The Battle of the Wilderness was the momentous beginning of a climactic epoch—the first clash between Lee and Grant and the beginning of what

The "Bloody Angle" at Spotsylvania Court House Battlefield. What happened here in May 1864 came to define the horror and intensity of the Civil War.

This early-twentieth century view of the Bloody Angle illustrates the early commemorative efforts that took place on this hallowed ground. (National Park Service)

would be the grinding road to Appomattox eleven months later. The harsh landscape of the Wilderness helped render the battle distinctively horrific: raging fires consumed swaths of the battlefield, along with hundreds of wounded. Those who saw it never forgot.

Days later, the armies clashed again around Spotsylvania Court House, scoring the landscape with miles of earthworks, signaling an inexorable shift in how wars would be fought. All of the anger and violence of war seemed to be unleashed in a single day—May 12, 1864—at the Bloody Angle, where, for twenty hours, Union and Confederate lines locked in savage combat, all of it face-to-face, some of it hand-to-hand. Like the Wilderness, Spotsylvania ended in stalemate. But Grant refused the verdict and continued onward, southward—toward Richmond, toward Appomattox.

Ellwood, a relatively simple plantation manor house built in 1790, was near the center of fighting during the Battle of the Wilderness in 1864. The family cemetery continues to be the resting place of General "Stonewall" Jackson's arm, buried here after amputation in 1863. Jackson later died from his wounds at nearby Guinea Station. (Scott Walker)

Sleepy Salem Church was the epicenter of fighting in 1863. Today, it stands along busy Route 3 as a testament to the war that once ravaged this entire area.

The ruins of circa 1816 Chancellor House, located within the Chancellorsville Battlefield. The site has been maintained by the National Park Service since the 1920s.

On May 21, 1864, the armies departed Spotsylvania County for the last time, leaving behind a trail of destruction, want, and discouragement that would take decades to heal. Portions of this land now comprise the Fredericksburg-Spotsylvania National Military Park.

www.nps.gov/frsp/

INDEX